Primary Grammar
and Punctuation
BOOK 2

Louis Fidge

Collins Educational
An imprint of HarperCollinsPublishers

Published by Collins Educational
An imprint of HarperCollinsPublishers Ltd
77-85 Fulham Palace Road
London W6 8JB

© Louis Fidge 1997

First published 1997

Reprinted 1998 (three times)

ISBN 0 00 302301 X

Louis Fidge asserts the moral right to be identified as the author of this work.

Illustrations by Rob Englebright, Bethan Matthews, Andrew Midgley,
Martin Remphry, Jakki Wood.

All rights reserved. No part of this publication may be reproduced, stored in a
retrieval system, or transmitted in any form or by any means, electronic,
mechanical, photocopying, recording or otherwise, without either the prior
permission of the Publisher or a licence permitting restricted copying in the
United Kingdom issued by the Copyright Licensing Agency Ltd,
90 Tottenham Court Road, London W1P 9HE.

British Library Cataloguing in Publication Data
A catalogue record for this book is available from the British Library.

Cover illustration: Rob Englebright
Editor: Gill Munton
Designer: Celia Hart

Printed by Scotprint, Musselburgh

Contents

Unit		Page
1	Parts of Speech (nouns, verbs and adjectives)	4
2	Common and Proper Nouns	6
3	Verbs (doing and being words)	8
4	Sentences and Phrases	10
5	Adjectives	12
6	Subjects and Verbs	14
7	Singular and Plural	16
8	Exclamation Marks	18
9	Verb Tenses (past and present)	20
10	Adverbs	22
	Progress Test A	24
11	Pronouns	26
12	Conjunctions	28
13	More about Adjectives	30
14	Prepositions	32
15	Adjectives (comparatives and superlatives)	34
16	Opposites (verbs)	36
17	Apostrophes (contractions)	38
18	Sentences (subject and predicate)	40
19	Direct Speech	42
20	Positive and Negative Sentences	44
	Progress Test B	46

UNIT 1 Parts of Speech
(nouns, verbs and adjectives)

Grammar is the study of the way in which we use words to make sentences. Words may be divided into groups called **parts of speech**. Three important **parts of speech** are **nouns**, **verbs** and **adjectives**.

The **powerful eagle landed**.

An **adjective** is a **describing** word. **Adjectives** tell us more about **nouns**.

A **noun** is a **naming** word. A **noun** can be the **name** of a person, place or thing.

Most **verbs** are words that describe actions. This **verb** tells us what **happened**.

Practice

Copy the sentences. Choose the most suitable verb to complete each sentence.

| caught | shouted | carried | crawled |
| planted | chased | sailed | typed |

1. The old turtle _____ up the hill.
2. The porter _____ the suitcases to our hotel room.
3. Mr Blake _____ some seeds in his garden.
4. The secretary _____ lots of letters.
5. Emma _____ at the top of her voice.
6. We _____ our boat out to sea.
7. The bull _____ the children across the field.
8. The eagle _____ the animal in its claws.

Making sure

1. Think of a suitable noun to go with each adjective.
   a) a red _____   b) the brown _____
   c) some golden _____   d) an empty _____
   e) a soft _____   f) the warm _____
   g) some tall _____   h) a foolish _____
   Now make up four sentences.
   Use one of your answers in each sentence.

2. Think of a suitable adjective to go with each noun.
   a) a _____ parcel   b) the _____ sea
   c) some _____ children d) a _____ wind
   e) a _____ accident   f) some _____ trees
   g) an _____ giant   h) the _____ books
   Now make up four sentences.
   Use one of your answers in each sentence.

Practise your punctuation

1. Punctuation marks make writing easier to understand. Punctuate these sentences correctly. Put in the capital letters, full stops, commas and question marks.

   a) the frightened child approached the dark castle
   b) what made that funny noise
   c) the small boy was carrying a big bag a book a pointed stick and an apple
   d) the old door creaked and opened
   e) a strange old lady stood in the shadows

2. In the sentences you have written:
   a) underline the verbs in red
   b) underline the nouns in blue
   c) underline the adjectives in green

UNIT 2 Common and Proper Nouns

A **noun** is the **name** of a person, place or thing.
Common (or ordinary) **nouns** are the **names** of people, places or things **in general**.
A **proper noun** is the **name** of a **particular** person, place or thing.

A **common noun** starts with a **small letter**.

The **boy** went by **train** from the **station**.
Tom went by **Eurostar** from **Waterloo**.

A **proper noun** starts with a **capital letter**.

Practice

Snow White	crocodile	bus	Fluff	Manchester
letter	Mr Barnes	house	shop	River Thames
The Times	day	Mars	pet	Sunday	word
woman	Easter	Nasir	sentence

Draw a chart like this. Write each of the nouns in the box in the correct column.

Proper nouns	Common nouns
Snow White	crocodile

6

Making sure

1. Copy the sentences. Underline the proper nouns. Circle the common nouns. The first one has been done for you.
   a) The (coach) to Birmingham was full.
   b) At Diwali some people have a party.
   c) The boat sailed down the River Severn.
   d) During his holiday Ben visited Portugal.
   e) Sir Francis Drake was a famous explorer.
   f) My favourite team is Chelsea.
   g) Mrs Rossetti is a keen gardener.
   h) The book was *The Pink Pyjamas* by Barbara Miller.

2. Now complete this alphabetical list of people and places.

Dont worry if you can't think of a name or place for every letter!

Andrew lives in America.
Billy lives in Bermuda.
Claire lives in Canada.

Practise your punctuation

1. Punctuate these sentences correctly.
   a) ann moore lives in edinburgh
   b) my address is 14 king street
   c) have you ever been to america canada mexico or jamaica
   d) the mountaineer climbed mount everest
   e) is christmas in november or december

2. In the sentences you have written:
   a) underline the common nouns
   b) circle the proper nouns

UNIT 3 Verbs (doing and being words)

Most **verbs** are words that describe actions.
They tell us what someone is **doing** or what is **happening**.
Some **verbs** are **being** words.

The frog **hops** into the water.

The frog **is** green and brown.

This is a **doing** verb.
It tells us what the frog is **doing**.

This is a **being** verb.
It tells us what the frog **is**.

Practice

1. Copy the sentences. Underline the **doing** verb in each one.
   a) Tadpoles nibble weeds.
   b) Tadpoles swish their tails.
   c) The frog jumped on to a rock.
   d) The frog croaked loudly.

2. Complete each sentence with the correct **being** verb from the box.

am	are	is	was	were	will be

   a) Tadpoles _____ baby frogs.
   b) I _____ too hot.
   c) Victoria _____ Queen of Britain.
   d) Ali _____ good at spelling.
   e) Tomorrow we _____ one day older.
   f) The Egyptians _____ inventive people.

Making sure

1. Copy the sentences. Choose the correct **doing** verb from the brackets to fill each space.
    a) If you _____ the ball I will _____ it. (catch/throw)
    b) Cork _____ on water but metal _____. (floats/sinks)
    c) A customer _____ things but a shopkeeper _____ them. (buys/sells)
    d) A captain _____ and the team _____. (leads/follows)
    e) The child _____ the heavy weight and then _____ it. (dropped/lifted)
    f) The woman _____ a hole and then _____ it in again. (filled/dug)

2. Copy the sentences. Underline the **being** verb in each one.
    a) Samir is a tall boy.
    b) The doctor was late.
    c) Tomorrow will be Sunday.
    d) The Vikings were good fighters.
    e) How are you today?
    f) I am tired.

Practise your punctuation

1. Punctuate the sentences in this story correctly.

    sooty looked up at the table hungrily the budgerigar was in its cage on the table the cat jumped up the bird was frightened mrs sharp heard all the noise and ran into the room she was very angry with the cat

2. In the sentences you have written:
    a) underline the **doing** verbs
    b) circle the **being** verbs

UNIT 4 Sentences and Phrases

A **sentence** is a group of words that **makes sense** on its own.
Every **sentence** must contain a **verb**.
A **phrase** is a group of words that **does not make sense** on its own.
Most **phrases** are **short**. Most **phrases do not** contain **verbs**.

The girls ran along the beach.

This is a **sentence**.
It **makes sense** on its own.
It contains a **verb**.

along the beach

This is a **phrase**.
It **does not make sense** on its own.
It **does not** contain a **verb**.

Practice

1. Which of the following are sentences? Which are phrases?
   List the sentences. Then list the phrases.
   a) A ghostly sea captain spoke to the girl.
   b) the silver fish
   c) The ship sank into the sea.
   d) The dog chewed the bone.
   e) this morning
   f) yes
   g) King Henry was fond of sport.
   h) The sun came out.
   i) Stand up.
   j) The girl ran out of the cave.

2. Now underline the verb in each sentence.

Making sure

1. Choose a suitable phrase from the box to complete each sentence.

| in its cage | because of the fog | through the town |
| over the wall | at night | after the rain |

a) The zoo keeper put the vulture back _____.
b) The soil was very wet _____.
c) Three girls climbed _____.
d) Owls come out to hunt _____.
e) The fire spread _____.
f) The football match had to be cancelled _____.

2. Make up six sentences. Include one of these phrases in each one.

| under the sea | down the hill | at midnight |
| outside the house | in the woods | because of the cold |

Practise your punctuation

Rewrite these pairs of sentences. Exchange the verbs in each pair so that the sentences make sense.

1. The lady laid an egg. The hen fried an egg.
2. The man boiled his scarf. The cook lost the potatoes.
3. Fishes trot. Horses swim.
4. The goat sang the grass. The girl ate the song.
5. The builder shaved the house. The man built his chin.
6. The teacher roasted her husband. The doctor kissed her chicken.

UNIT 5 Adjectives

An **adjective** is a **describing** word.
Adjectives give us more information about **nouns**.
Adjectives make sentences **more interesting**.

The dragon came out of the cave.
The **fearsome**, **fiery** dragon came out of the **huge**, **dark** cave.

We can improve the first sentence by adding some **adjectives**.

Practice

Copy the sentences. Choose the most suitable adjective from the brackets to fill each gap.

1. The _____ beggar wore _____ clothes. (poor, wet, dirty, new)
2. The _____ giant lived in an _____ castle. (ugly, cold, old, blue)
3. The _____ girl ate a _____ apple. (purple, little, juicy, hairy)
4. The _____ lady smiled as she sat on the _____ bench. (wooden, cheerful, red, rubber)
5. The _____ cat chased the _____ mouse. (fat, dry, noisy, tiny)
6. The _____ monster had a _____ nose. (wobbly, long, strange, metal)
7. The _____ clown tripped over his _____ boots. (funny, thin, heavy, big)
8. A _____ hedgehog walked up the _____ path. (narrow, high, prickly, quiet)

12

Making sure

1. Copy the sentences. Leave out the adjectives.
   a) The brave knight fought the fiery dragon.
   b) The mighty wind ripped up the old tree.
   c) Some green racing cars sped along the wide track.
   d) Where have the gigantic dinosaurs gone?
   e) The small wooden boat was tossed about by the rough sea.
   f) A strange little man with a pointed hat sang a sad song.

2. Copy the sentences. Put in some adjectives to make them more interesting.
   a) The dog ate the bone.
   b) The boy climbed the tree.
   c) A burglar forced the door open.
   d) A police officer chased the robber.
   e) The girl went out on her bike.
   f) The house was in the woods.

Practise your punctuation

Punctuate this passage correctly.
Each time you come to the adjective nice, replace it with a more interesting word.

saturday was a nice day youssef dressed in some nice clothes he called for alice she lived in a nice house they went for a nice walk in the park youssef bought a nice ice cream alice bought a nice bag of chips they played on the swings and had a nice time

Unit 6 — Subjects and Verbs

Every **sentence** has a **verb**. Every **sentence** also has a **subject**. The **subject** is the **main person or thing** in the **sentence**.

Scott saw an elf.

This is the **subject** of the **sentence**. The **subject** is usually found **in front of** the **verb**.

This is the **verb**. It tells us what Scott **did**.

Practice

Copy the sentences. Underline the subject and circle the verb in each one. The first one has been done for you.

1. <u>Sandra</u> (saw) a fairy.
2. Dogs bark.
3. Tortoises eat lettuce.
4. The helicopter crashed.
5. Eddie followed the strange troll.
6. Charlie found some gold.
7. The snake slid through the grass.
8. Sam won the race.
9. Curry is my favourite dinner.
10. Jack and Jill went up the hill.

Making sure

1. Think of a suitable subject to complete each sentence. Underline the verb in each sentence.

   a) _____ is a good friend.
   b) _____ swung through the trees.
   c) _____ hunt for food at night.
   d) _____ has lovely handwriting.
   e) _____ buried the treasure.
   f) _____ scared the children.

2. Think of a suitable sentence ending to go with each subject. Underline the verb in each sentence.

   a) The proud princess _____
   b) The submarine _____
   c) Humpty Dumpty _____
   d) A roaring dragon _____
   e) Some old people _____
   f) The strong wind _____

Practise your punctuation

1. Match the subjects and sentence endings. Punctuate the sentences you make correctly.

Subjects	Sentence endings
a) penguins	give us milk cheese butter and cream
b) little jack horner	has very sharp teeth
c) a shark	are black and white and live in the antarctic
d) the space monster	sat in the corner
e) gary stardust	had a pointed head and green teeth
f) cows	sang a pop song to the crowd

2. In the sentences you have written:
   a) underline the verbs
   b) circle the subjects

UNIT 7 Singular and Plural

We can write **nouns** in the **singular** or the **plural**.
Singular means **one**.   **Plural** means **more than one**.

one rattle   two rattle**s**   one bab**y**    two bab**ies**

We just add **s** to many **singular nouns** to make them **plural**.

When a **noun** ends in a **consonant + y** we change the **y** to **i** and add **es**.

Practice

Copy and complete this chart.

Singular	Plural
school	
fly	
	cars
	factories
city	
picture	
	walls
lorry	
	spies
lady	

Making sure

The **baby is asleep**.   The **babies are asleep**.

Take care when you change the **subject** of a sentence into the **plural**. The **subject** of the sentence and the **verb** must always agree.

1. Copy the sentences. Change the subject of each sentence into the plural. Make the verb agree with the subject.
    a) The fly is on the table.
    b) The door was open.
    c) The story is boring.
    d) The lorry was speeding.
    e) The dog is barking loudly.
    f) The factory has lots of windows.

2. Copy the sentences. Change the subject of each sentence into the singular. Make the verb agree with the subject.
    a) The pictures are very well painted.
    b) The families were sitting on the beach.
    c) The walls were very dirty.
    d) The ponies are galloping round the field.
    e) The cars are moving on to the ferry.
    f) The cities are full of heavy traffic.

Practise your punctuation

1. Copy the sentences. Make the verb in each sentence agree with the subject. Punctuate each sentence correctly.
    a) the pennies was in the purse
    b) some tigers is roaming through the trees
    c) a horse were eating a carrot
    d) the baby were drinking a bottle of milk
    e) lorries cars ships and aeroplanes is all means of transport
    f) ponies has manes

2. Now underline all the plural nouns in the sentences.

17

UNIT 8 Exclamation Marks

An **exclamation mark** is a punctuation mark.
This is an **exclamation mark**: !
An **exclamation mark** comes at the **end of a sentence**.
It shows that the writer feels **strongly** about something.

| ! can show **excitement** or **surprise**. | ! can give **warning**. | ! can show that someone is **hurt**. | ! can show that something happens **suddenly**. |

Practice

Which of these are exclamations? Which are questions?
List the exclamations. Then list the questions.

- Come here quickly!
- Where are you going?
- What is the time?
- How do they do that?
- Help! Im stuck!
- Look what I have found!
- Why are you sad?
- I feel quite dizzy!
- When can we go home?
- Smash! Bang! Crash!

Making sure

What do you think each person is saying? Write it down.
Remember the exclamation marks.

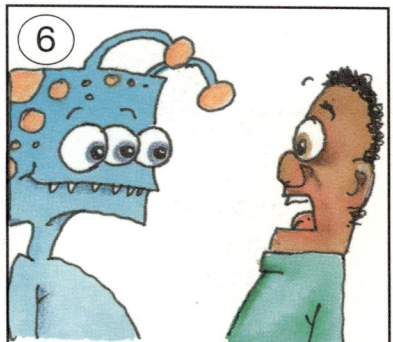

Practise your punctuation

Punctuate each of these correctly.

1. is it safe to open the door now
2. do not do that
3. come here
4. what do you think you are doing
5. hands up this is a robbery
6. what is for tea
7. that is a nasty cut
8. help I am trapped in the mud

UNIT 9

Verb Tenses
(past and present)

Verbs written in the **present tense** tell us what is happening **now**.
Verbs written in the **past tense** tell us what happened **in the past**.

Today Tom i**s rowing** his boat.   Last week Tom **rowed** his boat.

This **verb** is in the **present tense**. It tells us what is happening **now**. Verbs in the **present tense** often have **ing** at the end.

This **verb** is in the **past tense**. It tells us what happened **in the past**. Verbs in the **past tense** often have **ed** at the end.

Practice

Copy the sentences. Underline the verb in each one.
Show whether it is in the present tense or the past tense.
The first one has been done for you.

1. Ben <u>is finishing</u> his homework. (*present tense*)
2. Rosie is helping her mum.
3. Joe read a good book yesterday.
4. The mouse squeaked loudly.
5. On Saturday we walked to the shops.
6. The boy smiled at the girl.
7. On holiday I visited France.
8. The log floated down the river.
9. Emma is sitting in the sun.
10. The frog hopped on to the rock.

Making sure

jump	shout	talk	help	float	play
skip	hop		laugh	act	

1. Write a pair of sentences using each verb.
   In the first sentence, the verb should be in the present tense.
   In the second sentence, the verb should be in the past tense.
   The first one has been done for you.

   Today Sam is jumping.   Yesterday Sam jumped.

2. Copy and complete this chart.

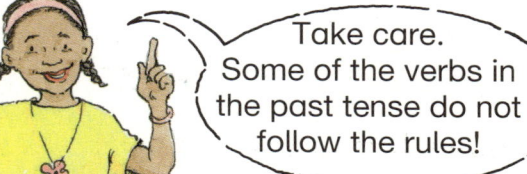

Take care. Some of the verbs in the past tense do not follow the rules!

Verb	Present tense	Past tense
wait	Tom is waiting	
skip		Tom skipped
cook	Tom is cooking	
catch	Tom is catching	
eat		Tom ate

Practise your punctuation

1. Punctuate each sentence correctly.
   a) the children are climbing a tree
   b) beth is sucking her thumb
   c) andy and dan are playing in the park
   d) I am writing a poem about a butterfly
   e) the dog is chasing the postman

2. Underline the verb in each sentence.

3. Rewrite each sentence, changing the verb into the past tense.

UNIT 10 Adverbs

An **adverb** is a word which gives **more meaning** to a **verb**.
Many **adverbs** tell us **how** something happened.

The sun shone **brightly**.

This is an **adverb**.
It tells us **how** the sun shone.

Many **adverbs of manner** (**how** adverbs) end in **ly**.

Practice

| carefully | quietly | crossly | soundly | noisily | quickly |

1. Complete each sentence with a suitable adverb from the box.
    a) I eat crisps _____.
    b) I listen _____.
    c) I sleep _____.
    d) I whisper _____.
    e) I run _____.
    f) I argue _____.

2. Copy the sentences. Underline the adverb in each one.
    a) The rain fell heavily.
    b) The river flowed rapidly.
    c) The boy spoke rudely.
    d) Shahla was dressed smartly.
    e) The time passed slowly.
    f) Cross the road safely.
    g) The girl sang loudly.
    h) The nurse treated me gently.

Making sure

1. Form an adverb from each adjective.
   The first one in each group has been done for you.
   a) deep ⟶ deeply
   b) light
   c) proud
   d) clever
   e) glad
   f) fierce
   g) clear
   h) slow

   i) humble ⟶ humbly
   j) noble
   k) gentle
   l) simple
   m) feeble
   n) horrible
   o) sensible
   p) terrible

   q) happy ⟶ happily
   r) angry
   s) heavy
   t) hungry
   u) lucky
   v) merry
   w) easy
   x) lazy

2. Copy and complete these adverb webs.

   a) 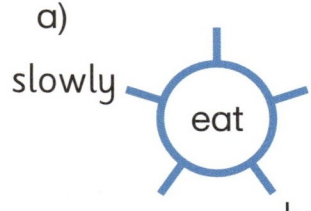 slowly ... eat ... hungrily

   b)  sing

   c) 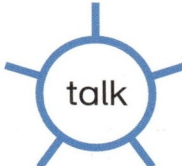 talk

Practise your punctuation

1. Punctuate this passage correctly.

   the children were throwing things running shouting and laughing what a noise mrs turner walked quickly down the corridor she stormed angrily into the room mrs turner shouted loudly the noise stopped suddenly the children slowly returned to their seats and got on quietly with their work

2. Now underline all the adverbs in the passage.

Progress Test A

1. Copy the sentences.
   Underline the **subject** in each one. Circle the **verb**.
   a) My brother plays loud music.
   b) Joanne sings very well.
   c) I am sailing my boat this morning.
   d) The passengers are boarding the bus.

2. Now write the sentences in the **past tense**.
   The first one has been done for you.

   Yesterday my brother played loud music.

3. Make up a **sentence** including each of these **phrases**.
   a) on the dinosaur   b) in the water   c) last night
   d) when the dragon   e) after a time   f) with a fork

4. Copy the chart, and write each **noun** in the correct column.

bird	Coronation Street	house	Mrs Finch	February
day	Jupiter	holiday	Fernbank Junior School	Holland
Diwali	mother	snow	Joanne	envelope	King John

Common nouns	Proper nouns

5. Think of a suitable **adverb** to complete each sentence.
   a) Mark behaved very _____.
   b) The crowd shouted _____.
   c) Last night the rain fell very _____.
   d) The elephant lumbered _____ along.

6. Copy and complete this chart.

Singular	Plural
sock	
shirt	
fly	
story	
dog	
baby	
boat	
swimmer	
army	
city	

7. Choose a suitable **adjective** from the box to make each sentence more interesting.

playful   tall   crowded   stormy   serious   bright

a) The puppy in the park was very _____ .
b) The car and the lorry were involved in a _____ accident.
c) The _____ trees in the forest made it seem very dark.
d) Tom was blinded by the _____ sunlight.
e) The _____ weather made the ferry crossing very unpleasant.
f) It was difficult to move because the streets were so _____ .

8. Copy the sentences. In each sentence, underline the **being verb** and circle the **doing verb**.
a) Alvin Moonburst is a pop singer who sings very well.
b) The Romans were good soldiers who fought bravely.
c) Dogs bark loudly but they are good pets.
d) The doctor came when I was unwell.
e) I am a good speller and score full marks in tests.
f) Toffees are my favourite sweets and I eat lots of them.

UNIT 11 Pronouns

A **pronoun** is a word which **takes the place** of a **noun**.

Fitzherbert knew that **Fitzherbert** was different from the others.
Fitzherbert knew that **he** was different from the others.

In this sentence we use the pronoun **he** instead of the noun **Fitzherbert**. This stops us from **repeating ourselves** and **sounds better**.

Practice

Copy these sentences. Use pronouns from the boxes to complete them.

1. The children were sad when _____ were told off.
2. Rachel said that _____ was fed up.
3. Do _____ like chips? Yes, _____ do!
4. Pass the ball to _____ , Tom shouted.
5. Katie asked Harry to give _____ a sweet.
6. When Dan got home _____ watched television.
7. Where is the ball? _____ is under the chair.
8. Come with _____ . _____ are going shopping, the girls said.
9. The birds flew away when the cat chased _____ .
10. Lisa smiled at Dan. _____ smiled back at _____ .

he, him

it

you

I, me

they, them

we, us

she, her

Making sure

Copy the sentences. Replace each of the underlined nouns with a pronoun. The first one has been done for you.

1. Pick up your book and put <u>your book</u> on the desk.
   Pick up your book and put it on your desk.
2. My sister and I are going on holiday because <u>my sister and I</u> like the sun.
3. Ben knew exactly what to do when <u>Ben</u> saw the robber.
4. When the girl walked in the rain <u>the girl</u> got wet.
5. Mrs Blake gave Tom a hug because <u>Mrs Blake</u> loved <u>Tom</u>.
6. The race was very important. <u>The race</u> turned out to be very exciting.
7. After the woman had read the book <u>the woman</u> returned <u>the book</u> to the library.
8. Ann and I spent the night at a hotel. <u>Ann and I</u> left the next morning.

Practise your punctuation

1. Punctuate these sentences correctly.
   a) we live in a big house with a large garage I keep a bike a sledge a go-kart and some footballs in it
   b) pull the rope hard if you let it go the post will fall over
   c) the television programme bored me it was very dull even the adverts were boring they were too old
   d) we went to the match mr smart gave us a lift
   e) joe asked mrs crown the way to the shop she told him how to get there
   f) give me an apple please

2. Now underline all the pronouns in the sentences.

Unit 12 Conjunctions

> A **conjunction** (sometimes called a **connective**) is a **joining** word.
> A **conjunction** is a word we use to **join two sentences together** to make one longer sentence.

The dragon went on a journey.
The dragon left the man to guard his treasure.

The dragon went on a journey **and** left the man to guard his treasure.

> We have used the conjunction **and** to join the two sentences.
> Notice how the second sentence has been changed slightly.

Practice

**Make each pair of sentences into one longer sentence.
Use either the conjunction** and **or the conjunction** but.

1. The gorilla looked fierce. It was really rather tame.
2. Jack went to the shop. He bought a comic.
3. The referee blew the whistle. The game began.
4. My favourite food is chips. You prefer baked beans.
5. The lion chased the zebra. It sprang on to its back.
6. It rained heavily. The game continued.
7. Mum grabbed her umbrella. She went out into the rain.
8. Gary did ten spellings. He got two wrong.

Making sure

1. Make each pair of sentences into one longer sentence.
   Use either the conjunction **because** or the conjunction **so**.
   a) I went to bed early. I was tired.
   b) I felt sick. We hurried home.
   c) It was raining. We could not go out.
   d) Dan washed his hands. They were dirty.
   e) Jack overslept. He was late for work.
   f) I want something to eat. I am hungry.
   g) The dog barked. A cat was coming.
   h) There was a fire. We shouted for help.

2. Copy the sentences. Underline the conjunction in each one.
   a) Mark kept on trying until he passed his driving test.
   b) I hurt my leg when I was playing football.
   c) You must wash up before you go to bed.
   d) I have felt ill since I ate the cake you made.
   e) I washed the car while you were asleep.

Practise your punctuation

1. Punctuate these pairs of sentences correctly.
   a) the haunted house was old it stood in the middle of a dark forest
   b) the footballer was injured he was taken to hospital
   c) the dragon was angry it was caught in a trap
   d) the man was lucky he won the lottery
   e) the wind was strong it blew down several trees
   f) the child was frightened he ran away to london

2. Now rewrite the pairs of sentences.
   Make them into one sentence.
   The first one has been done for you.

   The old haunted house stood in the middle of a dark forest.

UNIT 13 More about Adjectives

An **adjective** is a **describing** word.
Adjectives tell us more about **nouns**.
Adjectives make writing **more interesting**.

There were **three** cars.
The **second** car was an estate car.
Joe liked the **red** car best.
He was very **excited** when he bought it.

Numbers are often used as **adjectives**.

Adjectives can tell us the **order** of nouns.

Adjectives can add **colour**.

Adjectives can describe **feelings**.

Practice

1. Copy the sentences. Choose a suitable colour, number or order adjective to complete each one.
   a) I bought a bunch of _____ bananas.
   b) I won first prize and Billy won the _____ prize.
   c) Calum bought a bag of _____ cherries.
   d) It takes _____ people to make a quarrel.
   e) In autumn, _____ leaves fall from the trees.
   f) The swan was as _____ as snow.
   g) Sophie's skirt was as _____ as grass.
   h) There are _____ players in a football team.

Making sure

1. Find a suitable ending for each of these sentences.
   Write the sentences.
   a) I felt angry when ...
   b) Ali felt excited when ...
   c) Jane was jealous when ...
   d) At school I was bored when ...
   e) He felt brave because ...
   f) The small boy was lonely when ...
   g) Mrs Smith was worried because...
   h) The burglar was surprised when ...
   i) I would feel shy if ...
   j) The cat was curious when ...

2. Say which you think is better. Explain why.
   a) Being pleased or being delighted
   b) Being happy or being ecstatic
   c) Being interested or being fascinated

3. Say which you think is worse. Explain why.
   a) Being gloomy or being miserable
   b) Being annoyed or being furious
   c) Being scared or being terrified

Practise your punctuation

1. Punctuate these sentences correctly.
   a) have you ever felt lazy have you ever wanted to stay in bed all day
   b) dan felt happy he felt contented satisfied pleased and delighted all at the same time
   c) edward threw the ball at sue unfortunately it missed and hit the window crash mr clark appeared at the door looking very angry
   d) it was shireens ninth birthday she had invited four friends to her party sam nazma dan and dean all came

2. Now underline all the adjectives in the sentences you have written.

UNIT 14 Prepositions

A **preposition** is a word that tells us the **position** of one thing in relation to another.

These words are **prepositions**.

The alien had two curly horns **on** its head.
Between its eyes it had a pointed nose.
Under its nose was a large mouth with sharp teeth.

Practice

| into | between | behind | in | on | above | beside | under |

Copy the sentences.
Choose a suitable preposition from the box to complete each one.

1. The green alien is _____ the spacecraft.
2. The red alien is _____ the ladder.
3. The orange alien is climbing _____ the spacecraft.
4. The blue alien is _____ the spacecraft.
5. The yellow alien is _____ the spacecraft and the rock.
6. The purple alien is _____ the rock.
7. The pink alien is _____ the rock
8. The brown alien is flying _____ the rock.

Making sure

Think of a suitable preposition to complete each sentence.

1. Tara received a lovely present _____ her aunt.
2. John draped his coat _____ a chair.
3. The pirate gold was buried _____ the ground.
4. Mrs West turned off the light _____ her bed.
5. The car raced _____ the dog at great speed.
6. Jamal ran _____ the race track twice.
7. The robber threw the stone _____ the shop window.
8. The car crashed _____ the traffic lights.
9. The lottery money was divided _____ two winners.
10. The magician pulled a rabbit _____ his hat.

Practise your punctuation

1. Match these sentence beginnings and endings.
   Write the sentences. Punctuate them correctly.
   a) in march the farmer put a fence   off his horse
   b) jenny and jake sailed their boat   through the woods
   c) the jockey fell   round his field
   d) our dog smudge ran   into the icy water
   e) the swimmer dived   across the road
   f) on sunday ben walked his dog   down the river

2. Now underline the preposition in each sentence.

Adjectives
(comparatives and superlatives)

An **adjective** is a **describing** word.
When we compare **two** nouns we use a **comparative** adjective.
When we compare **three or more** nouns we use a **superlative** adjective.

The Moon is **big**.   The Earth is **bigger**.   The Sun is the **biggest**.

This is an **adjective**.

This is a **comparative adjective**.
Many comparative adjectives end in **er**.

This is a **superlative adjective**.
Many superlative adjectives end in **est**.

Practice

Copy and complete this chart.

Adjective	Comparative adjective	Superlative adjective
	smaller	smallest
new	newer	
slow		slowest
	faster	
		wildest
hard		
		longest
	rounder	
soft		
		sharpest

Making sure

1. Write the comparative and superlative forms of each adjective. The first one in each group has been done for you.

   a) wise → wiser → wisest   b) brave
   c) safe   d) pale   e) strange
   f) tame   g) white   h) large

   i) hot → hotter → hottest   j) big
   k) fat   l) red   m) sad
   n) wet   o) thin   p) slim

   q) busy → busier → busiest   r) heavy
   s) noisy   t) lucky   u) pretty
   v) happy   w) ugly   x) dry

2. Copy the sentences. Choose the correct comparative or superlative adjective to fill each space.
   a) A rhinoceros is fat. A hippo is _____ but an elephant is _____.
   b) Ann is pretty. Kim is _____ but Sam is _____.
   c) My rabbit is tame. My cat is _____ but my dog is _____.

Practise your punctuation

1. Punctuate these sentences correctly.
   a) gorillas live in africa they are taller stronger fiercer and heavier than humans
   b) the three aliens approached the red one was hairy and the blue one was hairier still but the purple one was the hairiest thing I have ever seen

2. In the sentences you have written:
   a) underline the comparative adjectives
   b) circle the superlative adjectives

UNIT 16 Opposites (verbs)

Opposites are words whose meanings are as **different** as possible from each other.

The bus driver **loaded** the luggage.

The bus driver **unloaded** the luggage.

These verbs have **opposite** meanings.
We can sometimes give a verb the opposite meaning by adding a **prefix** like **un** or **dis** to the **beginning** of the verb.

Practice

1. Write the opposite of each of these verbs by adding the prefix **un**. The first one has been done for you.
    a) wrap   unwrap
    b) pack
    c) dress
    d) do
    e) tie
    f) cover
    g) buckle
    h) bolt

2. Rewrite these sentences. Change each verb to give the sentence the opposite meaning.
    a) Maria packed her case on Saturday.
    b) Ahmed soon got dressed.
    c) The knight buckled his belt.
    d) The old lady unbolted the door.
    e) Sue unwrapped the present carefully.

Making sure

1. Write the opposite of each of these verbs by adding the prefix **dis**. The first one has been done for you.
   a) trust   distrust
   b) agree
   c) like
   d) obey
   e) connect
   f) please
   g) appear
   h) allow
   i) arm

2. Rewrite these sentences. Change each verb to give the sentence the opposite meaning.
   a) Suddenly, as if by magic, the fluffy white rabbit appeared.
   b) The football players all agreed with the referee.
   c) I really like sprouts.
   d) The plumber called to connect the water supply.
   e) Children always obey their parents!
   f) Tom knew just how to displease his teacher.
   g) The referee disallowed the goal.
   h) The bandits were soon disarmed.
   i) The police officer distrusted the shopkeeper.

Practise your punctuation

1. Punctuate these sentences correctly.
   a) mr barnes filled the watering can
   b) joe carra mark and shireen arrived on friday
   c) when did you sell that lovely picture
   d) mrs simons lost her purse in the grass
   e) the children whispered to each other
   f) the soldiers captured some spies

2. In the sentences you have written:
   a) underline the verbs
   b) change each verb to give the sentence the opposite meaning, and write the new sentence.

UNIT 17 Apostrophes (contractions)

An **apostrophe** is a punctuation mark. This is an apostrophe: '
We use an **apostrophe** to show that one or more **letters are missing**.
We sometimes join two words together and miss out some letters.
We call these words **contractions**. (**To contract** means **to shorten**.)

I'm bored.

This is a **contraction**.
I'm is short for **I am**.

Let's go shopping.

This is a **contraction**.
Let's is short for **let us**.

Practice

1. Write these out in full. The first one has been done for you.
    a) couldn't   could not
    b) haven't
    c) aren't
    d) isn't
    e) hasn't
    f) don't

| 'm is short for **am** | 's is short for **is** | 'll is short for **will** |
| 've is short for **have** | 're is short for **are** | 'd is short for **would** |

2. Write each of these next to its contraction.
    a) it is
    b) we are
    c) I have
    d) she would
    e) we will
    f) who is
    g) I am
    h) you have
    i) you are
    j) I would
    k) we have
    l) he is

Contractions
I'm   I've   I'd   he's   she'd   you're
we've it's   who's we're   you've   we'll

Making sure

1. Copy each sentence, writing complete words instead of contractions. The first one has been done for you.
   a) I've got a new bike.   I have got a new bike.
   b) I'm going to France.
   c) She's a good swimmer.
   d) It's no good. You'll have to try harder.
   e) We're having a great time.
   f) I'm sure you'd like it.
   g) We'll all do it together.
   h) It isn't fair.

2. Copy each sentence, writing a contraction where possible. The first one has been done for you.
   a) Do not do it!   Don't do it!
   b) I have not got any money.
   c) The tigers were not very fierce.
   d) I will call for you later.
   e) Who is that?
   f) We have scored two goals.
   g) I would help if I could.
   h) They are in bed.

Practise your punctuation

1. Punctuate this conversation correctly.

   emma: Ive got a good joke do you want to hear it
   edward: I hope its a good one
   emma: what do you call a camel with three humps
   edward: I dont know
   emma: humphrey
   edward: thats the worst joke youve ever told me

2. Now underline any contractions in the sentences you have written.

Hello. I'm Humphrey!

UNIT 18

Sentences (subject and predicate)

Every **simple sentence** can be divided into **two parts**: a **subject** and a **predicate**.

The chicken **laid an egg**.

This is the **subject** of the sentence. The subject is the **main thing** or **person**.

This is the **predicate**. The predicate is **the rest of the sentence**. It always contains a **verb** which tells us what is happening.

Practice

Match these subjects and predicates to make simple sentences. Write the sentences. The first one has been done for you.

1. The snake   bake bread.
2. A grey cat   visited the sick child.
3. Bakers   chugged out of the harbour.
4. Comedians   hid in Sherwood Forest.
5. Robin Hood   slithered through the grass.
6. My pet dog   jumped over our fence.
7. Some fishing boats   tell jokes.
8. The busy doctor   was chewing a bone.

The snake slithered through the grass.

Making sure

1. Copy these sentences. In each one, circle the subject and underline the predicate. Every predicate should have a verb.
   a) My youngest brother eats a lot of pizzas.
   b) The big black crow flew into the clear blue sky.
   c) A fierce wild dog snarled at the frightened boy.
   d) Three strong men pushed the car back on to the road.
   e) Some straggly sheep were grazing in the field.
   f) Kieran and Jayesh ran into the cave as fast as they could.
   g) The new dentist inspected my teeth.
   h) The teacher in the playground blew the whistle.
   i) A small fishing boat was battered by the huge waves.
   j) The metal robot moved with strange clanking sounds.

2. Now tick the verbs in the sentences you have written.

Practise your punctuation

1. Punctuate these sentences correctly.
   a) the hungry tiger pounced on sara
   b) the guide dog found the injured explorer on top of the icy mountain
   c) the police officer chased the young burglar
   d) a red sports car crashed into the back of the coach
   e) the dragon ate prince rupert for breakfast
   f) the wise old wizard turned tess into a toad

2. Rewrite the sentences, changing the subject in each. The first one has been done for you.

   Sara pounced on the hungry tiger.

UNIT 19 Direct Speech

When we write down the exact words that someone has spoken we call this **direct speech**.
We use **inverted commas** to mark the **beginning** and **end** of what the person said. These are inverted commas: " "

The waitress said, "**Here is your soup.**"

This is exactly what the waitress said.
Everything she said goes **inside** the **inverted commas**.

Practice

I would like some soup, please.

Which soup would you like?

What sort of soup have you got?

You can have tomato soup or vegetable soup.

I'll have the tomato soup.

I'll go and get it for you.

Copy these sentences, putting in the inverted commas.

1. The lady said, I would like some soup, please.
2. The waitress asked, Which soup would you like?
3. The lady replied, What sort of soup have you got?
4. The waitress said, You can have tomato soup or vegetable soup.
5. The lady said, I'll have the tomato soup.
6. The waitress replied, I'll go and get it for you.

Making sure

Copy the sentences, putting in what you think each person is saying.

1. The doctor asked, "_____"

   The child replied, "_____"

2. The man shouted, "_____"

   The woman shouted back, "_____"

3. Dan said, "_____"

   Lisa answered, "_____"

4. Mrs Franks asked, "_____"

   Joanne replied, "_____"

Practise your punctuation

Punctuate these sentences correctly.

1. the troll roared why are you walking on my bridge dan replied Im walking because I cant fly

2. the car mechanic said theres a problem with the steering wheel mrs monk asked can you mend it by saturday

3. mr ford said you can have hamburger pizza curry or fish fingers for tea john answered Ill have hamburger and chips please

4. the teacher asked where do you think youre going beth said Im going home for dinner

5. jo asked what do you call someone who has jelly and custard in their ears carra said I dont know jo smiled and said a trifle deaf

UNIT 20 Positive and Negative Sentences

A **positive** word or sentence is one that means **yes**.
A **negative** word or sentence is the **opposite**. It means **no**.

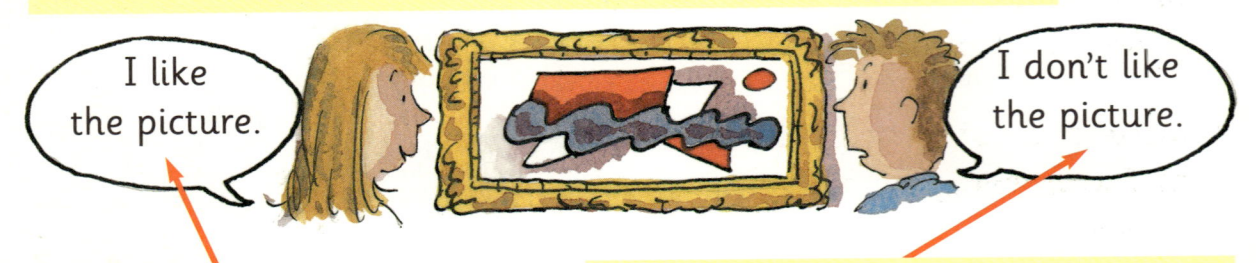

I like the picture.

I don't like the picture.

This sentence has a **positive** meaning.

This sentence has a **negative** meaning.
The main **negative** in English is **not** or **n't**.

Practice

1. Decide whether each sentence is positive or negative.
   The first one has been done for you.
   a) I am fond of spiders.   positive
   b) I can't finish this sum.
   c) I don't like swimming.
   d) The sun isn't very hot.
   e) Those animals are very tame.
   f) Paris is not in Scotland.
   g) Gary can't ride a bicycle.
   h) These questions are easy.
   i) Sasha is the best speller in the class.
   j) Camping is allowed in the forest.

2. Now rewrite each sentence, giving it the opposite meaning.
   The first one has been done for you.

   I am not fond of spiders.

Making sure

1. Make each of these sentences negative. You may need to change them a little. The first one has been done for you.
   a) The dragon blew smoke through its nostrils.
      The dragon did not blow smoke through its nostrils.
   b) Olivia plays the guitar.
   c) The fire burned for three days.
   d) The giraffe ate the leaves from the tree.
   e) Mr Jones caught the last bus home.

2. Make each of these sentences positive.
   a) The washing did not dry very well.
   b) Henry was not a king of England.
   c) Please don't wear your best clothes.
   d) The hedgehog does not hibernate in winter.
   e) It's not true!

3. What does each of these negative signs mean?
   a)   b)   c)   d)   e)

Practise your punctuation

1. Punctuate this passage correctly.
   rabbits do not come out to feed early in the morning they dont sleep during the day in their burrows their ears arent very long so rabbits cant hear very well they can not easily escape from their enemies because they are not able to run very fast rabbits dont have sharp front teeth they do not like nibbling carrots and lettuces

2. Now rewrite the passage using only positive sentences.

Progress Test B

1. Complete each of these sentences with a suitable colour, order or number **adjective**.
   a) There are _____ cars.
   b) The fourth car is _____.
   c) The _____ car is green.
   d) The third car is _____.
   e) The yellow car is _____.
   f) The fifth car is _____.

2. Copy each of these phrases and underline the **preposition**.
   a) playing in the park
   b) sitting on a chair
   c) running through the woods
   d) flying over the sea
   e) swimming under the water
   f) standing by a tree
   g) stopping outside a shop
   h) going up the stairs

3. Copy these pairs of sentences. Replace each of the underlined nouns with a suitable **pronoun** from the box. You can use each pronoun more than once.

them	it	him	they	she	her

   a) The boy could not carry the box. The box was too heavy for the boy.
   b) Mrs Bryant bought a new car. Mrs Bryant paid a lot for the new car.
   c) The firefighters fought the fire. The firefighters took a long time to put the fire out.
   d) Hannah keeps goldfish. Hannah feeds the goldfish every day.
   e) Sam and Ben have a dog called Sally. Sam and Ben take Sally for walks.

4. Make each pair of sentences into one longer sentence.
   Choose a **conjunction** from the brackets.
   a) Dad bought a new suit. It was too big for him. (and/but)
   b) It was an easy test. I finished it quickly. (if/so)
   c) I have a drink. I am thirsty. (and/when)
   d) You will be late for school. You do not hurry. (because/if)
   e) Sam picked an apple. She ate it straight away. (and/but)
   f) The lady put up her umbrella. It was raining. (until/because)

5. Copy these sentences. In each sentence, circle the **subject** and underline the **predicate**.
   a) My sister can stand on her head.
   b) Our classroom has thirty desks.
   c) The sun shone brightly all day.
   d) The flag was very colourful.
   e) Several horses galloped around the field.
   f) The big brown dog is barking furiously.
   g) Youssef wrote a good story.
   h) The noisy children were playing football.

6. Each of the sentences above is **positive**.
   Change each one into a **negative** sentence.

7. Copy and complete this chart.

Adjective	Comparative adjective	Superlative adjective
old		
long		
wet		
big		
large		
nasty		
hard		
white		
wet		

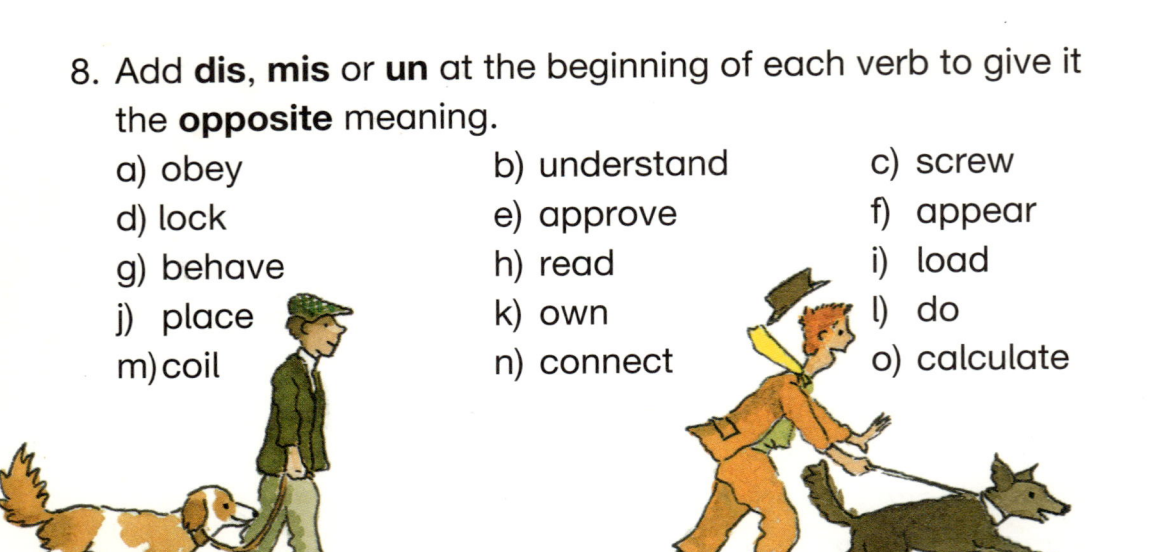

8. Add **dis**, **mis** or **un** at the beginning of each verb to give it the **opposite** meaning.
   a) obey
   b) understand
   c) screw
   d) lock
   e) approve
   f) appear
   g) behave
   h) read
   i) load
   j) place
   k) own
   l) do
   m) coil
   n) connect
   o) calculate

9. Match these sentence beginnings and endings.
   Write each sentence correctly.

   a) A phrase   is the main person or thing in the sentence.

   b) Every sentence   is used to compare two nouns.

   c) The subject   is a small group of words that does not make sense on its own.

   d) We use a plural   gives more meaning to a verb.

   e) The present tense of a verb takes the place of a noun.

   f) An adverb   when we are talking about more than one thing.

   g) A pronoun   tells us what is happening now.

   h) A comparative adjective   must contain a verb.